Doing Life With God

by

Bo Boshers

with Kim Anderson

Loveland, Colorado

This is EARL. He's R.E.A.L. mixed up. (Get it?)

Doing Life With God

Visit our Web site: **www.grouppublishing.com**

Credits

Editor: Amy Simpson

Creative Development Editor: Jim Kochenburger

Chief Creative Officer: Joani Schultz

Copy Editor: Lyndsay E. Bierce

Art Director: Kari K. Monson

Cover Art Director and Designer: Jeff A. Storm

Computer Graphic Artist: Nighthawk Design

Illustrator: Erica Andrews

Cover Photographer: Tony Stone, Inc.

Production Manager: Peggy Naylor

Library of Congress Cataloging-in-Publication Data

Boshers, Bo.

  Doing life with God / Bo Boshers.

    p. cm.

  ISBN 0-7644-2227-8

   I. Teenagers--Prayer-books and devotions--English. 2. Christian biography. I. Title.

BV4850 .B6367 2000

248.8'3--dc21

                      00-034086

10 9 8 7 6 5 4 3 2   09 08 07 06 05 04 03 02 01

Printed in the United States of America.

Acknowledgments

The thirty devotions in this book are real-life stories written by Christian high school students about how to give praise, be inspired, and find hope in difficult situations with God's help. I am grateful for their honesty and willingness to share their stories.

I'd also like to thank the youth ministers who helped find students interested in participating in this project. They serve in the following churches around the world: Westside Kings Church, Alberta, Canada; Shire Christian Centre, Sutherland, Australia; Flamingo Road Church, Fort Lauderdale, Florida; Willow Creek Community Church, South Barrington, Illinois; Christ Community Church, West Chester, Pennsylvania; Harbor Fellowship, Ontario, Canada; Central Baptist Church, Ponca, Nebraska; Hills Christian Life Centre, Sydney, Australia; Memorial Baptist Church, Evansville, Indiana; Concord Baptist Church, St. Louis, Missouri; Madison First Baptist, Madison, Tennessee; Rowandale Baptist Church, Manitoba, Canada; and Santa Cruz Bible Church, Santa Cruz, California.

In addition to the students and churches listed above, I'm thankful for the Willow Creek Association—for president Jim Mellado's vision and for the Association's commitment to provide training and resources to help churches prevail. A special thanks to Doug Yonamine for his support and willingness to answer all my questions.

Group Publishing is committed to making quality resources available for students. Thanks to Amy Simpson and the rest of the team for the work all of them did to make this book a reality.

Melissa D'Alexander and Brandy Ogata, two former Student Impact attenders now in college, provided creative writing and ideas for this book. Their contributions are appreciated and will make a difference in students' lives.

Thanks to my good friend Kim Anderson, who once again made my weaknesses look like strengths. Without Kim's patience, organization, and creativity, this project would not have been possible.

And to my children: Thanks Brandon, Trevor, and Tiffany for your prayers and advice on this project. I am so proud of all of you, and I love you. You are my heroes.

To my wife, Gloria: You are my best friend. Thank you for believing in me. Doing life with you is a gift from God. I love you.

4

Contents

Introduction **6**

Private Life

Not Ashamed 8

Why, God?. 11

A Turn From the Worst 13

A New Race 15

No Way Out 17

A Fresh Start 19

No Junk Here 22

Getting Off the Fence 24

Spiritual Life

Born a Christian?. 27

Reaching Out. 29

Praying for a Miracle 31

Standing on the Word 34

Speaking Up. 35

A Grateful Heart 38

Life on the Edge. 40

Staying on the Path 42

Home Life

If Only 46

Family Secrets 48

When the Storms Hit Home. 50

Choosing to Forgive 52

Amazing Grace 54

Phantom Father. 56

Social Life

Taking a Stand 59

Drawing the Line. 62

Real Friends. 64

Making Choices 65

Just Once. 68

Tired of Waiting 71

Three's a Crowd. 73

Out of Control 76

Tell Your Story
Tell Your Story 79

Introduction

Hi. My name is Tiffany Boshers, and I'm sixteen years old. I've been blessed to grow up in a Christian home and to be part of an awesome church. My family and my church have helped me grow in my relationship with Jesus Christ.

In the last few years, I've tried to grow in my personal relationship with Jesus by using some kind of devotional or study guide. I found out very quickly how difficult it is to find a devotional I can relate to and learn from.

Many of the books I read felt like homework assignments or bored me. I didn't really look forward to doing them. It seemed that these books defeated the whole idea of enjoying spending time with God.

I remember talking to my dad one day and telling him that I was trying to get closer to God by reading a devotional, but that none of the books I had found were holding my interest. Since my dad has worked in student ministry for almost twenty years, I asked him about an idea I had to let students tell their own stories instead of having an adult tell them to us.

I'm excited that my idea helped lead to the creation of this book of devotions. Every devotion in this book was written by students for students to help us develop our relationship with God. As you read these real-life stories that have come out of the personal experiences of Christian students around the world, I think you'll agree with me that God is powerful!

Some of the stories you read will relate directly to your life. You'll be encouraged by what God did to change a student's life and how he can change yours, too. Other stories will remind you of how God has protected you and been good to you. Perhaps a few of the stories will even challenge you to help a friend facing a tough situation.

But most of all, you'll be reminded, as I was, that you aren't alone. Students all over the world are trying to take a stand for God—students like you and me who understand how challenging it can be to fit in, make choices that honor God, get along with parents and siblings, and grow spiritually.

I pray this book gives you hope, inspiration, and encouragement as you take steps to grow in your personal relationship with God. Thanks, Dad, for listening to my need and helping me (as you always do) in my attempts to be fully devoted to Christ. I love you, Dad!

How to Use This Devotional

You may have read devotionals that are organized by specific dates. You turn to the devotion for a particular day, hoping for words of encouragement. But what if that devotion doesn't apply at all to what you're dealing with at that moment? It can be discouraging and cause you to lose interest.

This book is organized by topic so you can find issues you or a friend may be facing and read about other students who went through similar situations. Each devotion is written to help you learn life lessons through the choices (some good, some bad) made by other Christian students.

Here are the four main sections in *Doing Life With God:*

• **Private Life**—the private areas in your life that challenge and strengthen your character

• **Spiritual Life**—doing life with God and growing in your faith

• **Home Life**—the struggles and joys in relating to family

• **Social Life**—the issues you face with peers

Each devotion includes the following elements:

• **A Student's Story**—a story about God's working in a student's life

• **What God Taught Me**—powerful lessons God taught the student and key Bible verses for you to study

• **Write Your Story**—a chance for you to reflect on your own story and write down your thoughts through a journal exercise

• **Talk to God**—a suggested prayer you can use as you talk to God

• **Talk With Friends**—three questions related to the story for you to discuss with a few friends or in a small-group setting

Consistently connecting with God by reading a devotion each day will deepen your personal relationship with him and give you wisdom and strength to face each day.

As you read this book, you may feel you have a story that needs to be told. Well, if that's the case, send it in or e-mail it! The addresses are in the back of the book on page 79. The next volume of student devotionals is in progress, and we're looking for stories. Why not yours? It would be great to read your story and hear how God is working in your life.

My prayer is that these devotions will give you hope, inspiration, and encouragement to strengthen your relationship with God. Remember, being a Christian is awesome. Other Christian students around the world are fighting the same fears and temptations that you are. You aren't alone—keep fighting the good fight, dream big for God, and be a difference-maker today.

Private Life

Not Ashamed

Sara's Story

My parents are Christians, and I trusted Jesus at an early age. All my life, my family has been different from non-Christian families. The differences were small in elementary school, but they were enough that I remember occasionally feeling dumb and embarrassed about my faith. I specifically remember being embarrassed when filling out a typical "What is your favorite..." survey one day at school. I copied what my friends wrote for the "favorite TV actor" category because my family didn't watch TV enough for me to know what was cool.

In junior high, the differences grew slightly. Dirty language became the norm, gossip escalated, and junky movies were typical topics of conversation. I felt weird knowing more about David and Goliath than I did about the hottest TV star.

Once I reached high school, the differences between my beliefs and what the world was throwing at me were huge. I felt God was fine for young kids and adults, but he didn't cut it in high school. I became embarrassed about God. I envied the lifestyle of those around me. I made a deal with God: "Just let me live a non-Christian life for a while, God. Then I'll come back. And anyway, God, I deserve to see what it's like since I've been a Christian my whole life." And so I exchanged the truth for a lie.

I traded my Christian friends for older, "cooler" ones. I replaced my first love, God, for a cheap substitute, compromising many of my standards of purity. I even dipped my toes into the water of the drug scene. And because God will not come uninvited, he honored my requests and let me be. But the Holy Spirit continued to regularly bug my conscience. All the things I had once thought would be so great and thrilling were only giving me trouble, a restless spirit, and an empty feeling. I knew I needed God back in my life.

The summer after my freshman year, I worked at a Christian camp, where it was easy not to feel embarrassed about God. I made a commitment at that camp that I would fully live what I claimed to be. When my sophomore year began, I made the hard choice not to be part of certain crowds, but I still struggled with envy over my friends' seemingly exciting lifestyle.

Throughout the year, God reminded me that the broad path may look fun, but it ends in destruction.

During my junior year, I began to learn about and exercise my spiritual gifts and found out that I had a unique contribution to make in God's church. Yet despite all my spiritual growth, I continued to wrestle with the embarrassment I felt at school with my friends. My friends knew I was a Christian, but instead of being bold with my faith, I would compromise to fit in. The compromises seemed to be small, such as the music I listened to or the language I used or the type of people I hung around with. But even these small things filtered into me and resulted in an output of swearing, gossip, and the temptations to smoke and date non-Christians. It's not that Jesus wanted me to live in a bubble where I wouldn't encounter anything bad. He gave me choices and let me make my own decisions.

Finally, God broke through. After my junior year, I spent several weeks of the summer on service projects in the inner city and on an international missions trip. By serving others, being in a community with Christians, and spending time in solitude, I learned a lot about God's character. The ways of the world finally started to lose their appeal. It was then, after I truly experienced God's love, grace, and goodness, that God naturally flowed out of my life and began to help me share my faith with my friends with confidence.

"But as for me, it is good to be near God. I have made the Sovereign Lord my refuge; I will tell of all your deeds" (Psalm 73:28).

The embarrassment about my faith disappeared as I started to build real friendships and to tell my friends about God. I had never been so unashamed of my relationship with God in my whole life! God began to use me to work in my friends' lives. One of my friends committed her life to Jesus this year! I now know what an exciting life I can live as a Christian, walking and growing with God daily and being used to help change lives around me. What I had thought was the more fulfilling and desirable lifestyle can't even compare to my life now.

What God Taught Me

- God stayed faithful to me. God is good and gracious.
- God didn't give up on me when I was embarrassed about my faith.
- God listens to my prayers.
- God gives me strength, confidence, and wisdom when I need it.

Write Your Story

Can you relate to Sara's story? Have you ever felt embarrassed about your faith? Write down four steps you can take to have a stronger witness at your school.

Talk to God

Use this prayer, or use your own words to talk to God.

Jesus, sometimes it's hard for me to stand up for you at school. It seems easier to just go with the flow. But I know that you desire for me to follow the path you show me in the Bible. Please give me the courage to make decisions that honor you. Amen.

Talk With Friends

Discuss these questions in a small group:

• How are Christians viewed by the other students at your school?

• Would you or have you compromised your values and beliefs in order to hang out with certain groups at school? Explain.

Read Romans 1:16a together: "I am not ashamed of the gospel, because it is the power of God for the salvation of everyone who believes." How true is this verse in your life? Please explain..

• How comfortable do you feel talking about God with your friends? Why?

Why, God?

Brooke's Story

The phone rang, and my mom picked it up. I watched the tears well in her eyes as she slowly put the phone down. Her face was filled with fear.

"I have cancer," she said.

My mind raced with a bunch of questions and doubts. I tried to comfort my mom but had no understanding of what was happening. I was in shock. I had so many questions for God: Why was this happening to my mom? What did she do to deserve this? I was hurt and angry at God for letting this happen to my family.

My mom had to go to the hospital a week later for a major operation that would determine if she needed to go through chemotherapy. As I said goodbye to her the morning of the surgery, it crossed my mind that this might be the last time I would see her this healthy. I started to cry. I was trying to act strong for my mom, but I couldn't. She tried to reassure me that she would be all right, but it was so hard to leave her.

As I arrived home that night, I went straight to my room and cried hard and long. I was scared about the future, and I felt alone and helpless.

I wasn't allowed to see my mom the next day because my dad thought it would be too hard for me. I saw her the following day and just sat by her bed and watched her. It was a week before the results came in, and as we waited for them each day, I was more and more afraid.

> "Consider it pure joy, my brothers, whenever you face trials of many kinds, because you know that the testing of your faith develops perseverance" (James 1:2-3).

Well, you're probably wondering how my mom's test results turned out. By God's grace and goodness, the doctors were able to remove all the cancer from my mom's body during surgery. I don't know how my mom's health will be in the future, but I am so grateful that God spared her life. God is so good to me.

What God Taught Me

• God has everything in my world under control. I can trust in his sovereign plan and awesome power.

• God is trustworthy.

• God teaches me valuable life lessons through tough times.

• The Bible has taught me a lot about God's character and who he is.

Write Your Story

What are the trials in your life that are making you anxious? As you write your story, tell God exactly what you're feeling. Remember that he is in control and can handle any trial you're facing. Let God know exactly what you need to trust him with.

Talk to God

Use this prayer, or use your own words to talk to God.

Jesus, thank you for loving me enough to understand my anxious thoughts. Place people in my life who I can talk to about my concerns. Give me friends who will encourage me and lead me closer to you. Grant me understanding and patience to see your plan for my life. Amen.

Talk With Friends

Discuss these questions in a small group:

• What in your life makes you worried or concerned? Do these struggles make you angry with God or draw you closer to him? Why?

• In what ways has God been faithful to you in the past?

• What is one way you can be reminded that God is in control of your life?

A Turn From the Worst
Josh's Story

I've attended church for as long as I can remember, but I definitely haven't always lived my life according to God's plan. For a long time, I had my own set of rules. At the last church I attended, I found friends who were just like me. They got into drinking and drugs, and so did I, even though I knew in my heart that these choices were wrong and destructive.

I really got into this kind of lifestyle. For three years it seemed that all I ever did was drink and do drugs. I wrecked my truck and lied about it, telling my parents I was tired when in truth I was drunk. I even tried to commit suicide by attempting to jump off a balcony.

Most weekends, I would go out and look for a fight. I often hurt people pretty badly. I even used knives and cut people. I was able to put on an act at church and around my family. No one knew the terrible things that were going on in my life.

I fought hard with my parents about going to church. I didn't want to keep going because I didn't want to change. But deep down, I was scared. I really did want a clean slate and to make some changes in my life. At church, I met a few people who actually cared about me. They reached out to me and demonstrated God's love. I often thank God for bringing these people into my life because they led me to Jesus. I can't even imagine where I would be today if it weren't for God's intervention and amazing grace. I would probably be dead or in prison.

> **"If we confess our sins, he is faithful and just and will forgive us our sins and purify us from all unrighteousness" (1 John 1:9).**

My life has changed radically. My family can see a big difference in how I live and treat others. I'm much closer to my parents now. I've stopped drinking and doing drugs. I haven't been in a fight since I became a Christian. The temptations are not gone, but with God's help I'm able to overcome them one by one. Now if I feel angry or confused or sad, I talk to God and ask for help and strength.

What God Taught Me

- God forgives my wrongs and can give me a fresh start.
- God gives me courage and strength to overcome any obstacle.
- I can trust God to lead me every step of the way.
- God can rescue me from any temptation I face if I ask him for help.

Write Your Story

God has the power to change a human heart, to turn it from evil ways to his ways. Let God know which areas of your life you need help changing.

Talk to God

Use this prayer, or use your own words to talk to God.

Jesus, I pray that you'll strengthen me enough to depend on you for help in the midst of my temptations. I desire to live my life for you and only you. Thank you for rescuing me so often. Amen.

Talk With Friends

Discuss these questions in a small group:

• What kinds of struggles or temptations are you currently facing?

• What are some ways God has shown you his strength and wisdom in fighting temptation?

• Have you ever known a person who was addicted to drugs or alcohol? How did you help this person? If no one comes to mind, what would you say or do if the situation ever arose?

A New Race

Carly's Story

I'll never forget the state swimming tournament a few years ago. I had spent a lot of time training and preparing for it, practically living at the pool for weeks. When the day of the tournament arrived, I was so excited, as were the other three girls on my team. I was the second swimmer in a relay. I had never represented our district before. My mom and dad were all set with the video camera—they were so proud of me.

The moment for our relay arrived, and my heart was racing. The gun went off, and the first swimmer on my team kept the lead the whole way. When it was almost my turn, I stepped up to the block and put my goggles on. I crouched into position, waiting to see my teammate's hand on the wall. When her hand was within inches of the wall, I took off. As I swam, it crossed my mind that I might have hit the water before the other girl's hand touched the wall, but I was too excited to think negatively. I swam faster than I ever had before.

When the race was over, we huddled together to look at the results on the scoreboard. We had come in first and had broken the record for the fastest time! We couldn't believe it; we beat the other eight teams. As we cheered and jumped around, an official came over to us, interrupting our celebration. I'll never forget what he said: "Disqualification in lane four; the second swimmer dived in before the first swimmer hit the wall."

It's hard to describe just how I felt at that moment. I had disappointed everyone who believed our team could win, even myself. I felt the lowest I had ever felt in my life. I knew I had let my teammates down.

I continued swimming for four months. Then one day I decided I didn't want to swim anymore. I couldn't get over my failed performance, and I thought I was a failure too. I lived with despair and disappointment in myself for the next two years until I learned about God.

I knew something was missing in my life, and I was searching for answers to fill the void. Over time, I finally realized that God was the answer and could fill the emptiness in my soul. I knew that I

> **"Forgetting what is behind and straining toward what is ahead, I press on toward the goal to win the prize for which God has called me heavenward in Christ Jesus" (Philippians 3:13b-14).**

needed to depend on him in my everyday life. I made the decision to begin a personal relationship with God.

Eventually, God gave me the courage and confidence to compete in the same event again. I was the first swimmer this time, and our team came in third. That day, I got more than a second chance to swim a race; I got a fresh start. God has given me back hope and courage. God is good!

What God Taught Me

- God accepts me for who I am, even when I feel like a failure.
- I'm precious to God.
- Nothing I've ever done can prevent God from loving me.
- Trials test my faith and help me develop perseverance.
- God can handle anything. I can trust in him and lean on his love. God gives me hope to press on.

Write Your Story

God can turn disappointments into opportunities. How does this story remind you that God is faithful? Think of a time God helped you through a disappointment. Take a moment to thank him or let him know where you need his help.

Talk to God

Use this prayer, or use your own words to talk to God.

Jesus, I believe you can restore me and set me free from all my disappointments. Things don't always go my way, but I'm thankful that you're by my side and can help me overcome any obstacles. Give me the strength I need to face each day and to never lose my hope in you. Amen.

Talk With Friends

Discuss these questions in a small group:

• What's one disappointment you've had in the past year?

• How has God taken a disappointment and turned it into a learning experience?

• How do you think God sees you? How would your confidence change if you saw yourself as God does?

No Way Out

Samantha's Story

I had just turned fifteen, and summer was starting. I was making new friends from my church, and things in my life were going great. One Friday night, I went to a concert with some friends. After the concert, I had planned to stay over at a friend's house. I knew something was wrong, though, when my mom called and told me that plans had changed. She came and picked me up right away. She took me to a park, held my hand, and asked me to sit down next to her at a picnic table.

Then she said three words that changed my life: "Samantha, Brian's dead."

After I got over the initial shock, I broke down, sobbing as if my heart were actually breaking. Brian had been a good friend of mine. Through tears, I asked how he had died. I wasn't prepared for her answer: "He committed suicide."

The next few days were a blur. I spent that first night at my best friend's house because I couldn't bear to be alone in my bedroom all night. We cried a lot, listened to sad songs, and tried to talk about how we felt. We were mostly confused because Brian had always been so cheerful. He didn't seem like a person who would kill himself. It didn't seem real.

The funeral came, and all I remember was being so numb I could hardly cry. I held hands with two friends for almost the entire service and finally broke down when the song "Lord of Eternity" was played. I knew Brian had been strong in his belief in God because we had often talked about Jesus and how he was working in our lives.

> "Do you not know? Have you not heard? The Lord is the everlasting God, the Creator of the ends of the earth. He will not grow tired or weary, and his understanding no one can fathom. He gives strength to the weary and increases the power of the weak" (Isaiah 40:28-29).

I went through the normal grieving emotions, moving from guilt to shock to depression to anger. My friends and I became much closer, and I got a phone call a day from each of them for about a month. But when I was alone and the phone wasn't ringing, I felt a strong sense of hopelessness. I felt that nothing mattered because Brian was gone. Hopelessness consumed my thoughts, and I became despondent. I wrote poems, trying to sort through my emotions.

At a church summer camp I finally gave all my sorrows over to God. I told him that they were his because I couldn't handle them alone. I soon felt as if a weight had been lifted from my shoulders and from my heart. Over the next month or so, I felt God changing me and healing me—something I never could have done on my own.

What God Taught Me

- God taught me not to take people for granted.
- God loves me tremendously.
- God is much bigger than any problem I face, and he's willing and able to help me.
- God brought hope back into my life, as he always does if we trust him and hand all our problems to him.

Write Your Story

Sometimes the struggles we're facing can seem overwhelming, and we wonder how we can overcome them. It's good to be reminded that God can handle any problems that come our way. Take some time to thank him for being powerful and available.

Talk to God

Use this prayer, or use your own words to talk to God.

Jesus, you know how hard life can be. When you lived on earth, you encountered tough challenges too. Please give me the strength I need to face each day. Help me place my hope in you when times are difficult. Thank you for being a strong and faithful friend. Amen.

Talk With Friends

Discuss these questions in a small group:

• What do you do when you are discouraged? What helps you through tough times?

• If someone you knew talked about suicide, what would you do or say?

• How do you find God's love in tough times?

A Fresh Start

Jessica's Story

By the time I turned fifteen, I had been a Christian for two years. Although adults would often comment on how faithfully I served God, I felt anything but faithful on the inside. In fact, I felt pretty messed up.

My family attended a small church, and we became friends with a man named John. John's work brought him to our town, but his wife and two children were living elsewhere. We became like a second family to him.

One night, John offered to drive me to pick up a computer I had purchased.

Before driving back home, we took a walk around a romantic harbor, and he made me feel beautiful and special. He taught me how to kiss that night.

From that point on, our relationship grew, resulting in lies, confusion, and pain. During this time, John often told me that he loved me and that he was planning to divorce his wife to marry me. As I look back at this situation, I realize how empty his words were and how blind I was to his lies.

John took me to a motel a couple of times, but he was afraid to take any risks sexually. Although I'm grateful that I didn't lose my virginity, those times with him in the motel room made me feel guilty and impure. I knew our relationship was wrong, but John's lies were so reassuring that he convinced me our behavior was OK. I became more and more confused.

> " 'Come now, let us reason together,' says the Lord. 'Though your sins are like scarlet, they shall be as white as snow; though they are red as crimson, they shall be like wool' " (Isaiah 1:18).

The thing I hated most was lying to my family so I could spend time with John. I also felt guilty about the pain John's family would experience if they found out about us. I wanted out, but I felt trapped inside the situation, and I didn't know where to search for an exit.

Eventually my mom found out about John. When she asked me about our relationship, I poured out my heart and told her the truth. I continually thank God for how understanding and supportive she was through it all. Strangely enough, this regrettable experience has brought me closer to God.

My relationship with John left me full of hurt, guilt, and confusion. But after praying with my mom and another woman from our church, I felt that all the windows of my heart had been opened wide. The curtains fluttered as the purifying winds of God's love blew through me. I felt cold and exposed because my secret had been discovered, but I also felt free. I knew that was a new beginning and a fresh start.

What God Taught Me

- Reading the Bible daily helped me grow stronger in my relationship with God and pointed me in the right direction.

- My mom and other adults were there to help. If you feel trapped or sexually pressured by someone, don't hesitate to tell a Christian adult who can help you!

- It is important to talk to God about everything. If you find yourself facing a situation you feel like you can't escape, talk with God about it.

- God loves me, but God hates anything that separates me from him.

- God's love and forgiveness made me whole and enabled me to truly forgive John for his deceit. God's love and forgiveness are available to you, too. He can make you free and whole again no matter what you've done or what you feel trapped by. God can heal you.

Write Your Story

We all have areas in our lives where the issue of purity is in question, such as the kinds of magazines we read, TV shows or movies we watch, words we use, or ways we act on dates. Know that God promises to wash us white as snow if we repent and confess to him. What are the areas in your life that need some washing? Share them with God here.

God, I want a clean and pure heart. Help me with…

Talk to God

Use this prayer, or use your own words to talk to God.

Jesus, I know that sometimes I make choices that don't honor you. Please forgive my impure heart and wash me white as snow. Teach me to be more like you and to follow the truths in your Word. Amen.

Talk With Friends

Discuss these questions in a small group:

• What does God mean when he talks about washing you "as white as snow" (Isaiah 1:18)?

• In what areas of your life do you make choices that sometimes lead you away from a pure heart: TV? movies? magazines? music? the Internet?

• What's one step you could take to change these patterns?

No Junk Here

Kari's Story

Junior high was one of the hardest times of my life. Every day was worse than the one before. A lot of kids bothered me in school, mainly because I matured faster than everyone else did. They would say mean things about me, such as, "Look at the obese girl. You're so stupid. You're ugly." At that age I was still trying to figure out where I belonged, so I took whatever people said about me seriously and started to believe it. All I ever heard from some kids was how bad I was and that no one would ever want to be friends with me. I had a few friends who told me not to listen to those kids because everything they said was a lie, but my friends' words didn't encourage me. I cried nearly every night after I'd gotten home.

My parents tried to make me feel better. They told me that the other kids were jealous of me and that's why they bothered me. My response was: What could they possibly be jealous of? What do I have that they don't? I let the kids bother me so much that I went into a deep depression. I would lock myself in my room blasting my music or hide in my closet under the clothes so no one could find me. I was always dazed at school, and I shut myself off to everyone. When kids teased me, I in turn bullied smaller or weaker kids to try to deal with the emotional pain. My self-esteem was incredibly low.

After a year and a half, I was fed up with my

"O Lord, you have searched me and you know me. You know when I sit and when I rise; you perceive my thoughts from afar. You discern my going out and my lying down; you are familiar with all my ways. Before a word is on my tongue you know it completely, O Lord…I praise you because I am fearfully and wonderfully made; your works are wonderful, I know that full well" (Psalm 139:1-4, 14).

life and felt that I had no purpose. I attempted suicide by slitting my wrists. I didn't succeed. I couldn't believe what I had tried to do, so I didn't tell anyone until just recently. Two days after my attempted suicide, I went to church as usual, as if nothing had happened. I don't remember what the pastor said at all. All I can remember is that there was an opportunity to become a Christian, and I could feel God tugging at my heart. I knew I wanted my life to change and I needed God's help. I was crying out for help.

I'll never be able to fully explain what happened that day, except to say that it changed my life forever. My heart had been so torn up that I felt as if I had no heart at all until God took the broken pieces of my life and mended them, giving me a new heart.

My self-esteem continues to get stronger. I can now look in the mirror and like who I see.

What God Taught Me

• God taught me so much about himself and who he made me to be. He started to heal my heart and show me how very much he loves me.

• I now try to think about how God sees me instead of what other people think. I'm a precious child of God, and God sees me as his beloved.

• God is ready to listen to whatever I want to tell him. I need to talk with him and share my feelings.

Write Your Story

Take a few minutes to rewrite the verses in the box on page 22 in your own words. Try substituting your name every time "I" or "me" is used.

Talk to God

Use this prayer, or use your own words to talk to God.

Jesus, you made me, and you know everything about me. Your love for me never wavers. Thank you for being faithful to me and for not changing. Show me who I am through your eyes. Amen.

Talk With Friends

Discuss these questions in a small group:

• Have you ever felt really down or known someone who was? What did you do to help yourself or that person?

• If someone you know ever talked about suicide, what would you say about God that would show them he cares and understands?

• What are some ways you can encourage a friend to seek out God's love?

Getting Off the Fence
Brian's Story

I had always heard other people's stories about their awesome experiences with God—stories about feeling God at work, guiding them in their everyday lives. At a conference I attended last summer, the speakers said that if I, too, really wanted to experience God, I had to listen carefully for God's voice and look at everyday circumstances. They told me that to know God's voice, I had to know God's Word.

I hadn't read the Bible before on a regular basis, but I definitely wanted to grow in my spiritual life and experience God. I was sick of being just a lukewarm Christian. I had gone to church all my life and had all the Sunday school answers, but I felt stuck in my relationship with God. I wanted to see God work in my life and use me for his purposes. I knew it was time for me to get off the fence and live totally for God.

At the conference, I was also challenged to get out of my comfort zone. True faith requires action! I decided that week that I didn't want to stay where I was.

I started reading the Bible every day. Once I started reading, I was amazed at how interesting and relevant the Bible is. I found some really powerful verses. I prayed and told God I wanted to get to know him better. I told him I was ready to be used and I wanted to make a difference for him.

During that time, I had a friend in Australia. We wrote back and forth to each other via e-mail almost every day. One day, she sent me an e-mail about religion. She told me she didn't believe in any specific religion, but she believed different parts of various religions. Then at the end, she asked me what I believe.

I was so excited! Here was a chance to share my faith and get out of my comfort zone! It was an answer to prayer. I didn't want to waste this opportunity, so I told her what I believe. I told her how I became a Christian and said that if she ever had any questions, she could ask me. I didn't know all the answers, but with the help of my youth pastor, I wrote back and tried to help her with her questions. I don't know how it will turn out, but the opportunity to share my faith is so exciting.

> **"Let us not become weary in doing good, for at the proper time we will reap a harvest if we do not give up" (Galatians 6:9).**

I regularly pray that my friend will continue to be interested in hearing more and that God will give me the right words to say. I know for sure that this past summer has changed my life. I've experienced God in ways I had never thought possible.

What God Taught Me

- I need to step out of my comfort zone so God can use me for his purposes.
- God loves me and is always there for me, no matter what.
- I can pray and talk to God about the challenges and joys in my life.
- Being a lukewarm Christian isn't the way to live life to the fullest. By living fully for God and being open to the opportunities he brings my way, I experience incredible joy and know that my life has real purpose.

Write Your Story

Can you relate to Brian's story? Have you ever found yourself living a lukewarm Christian life? Tell God in your own words how you feel.

Talk to God

Use this prayer, or use your own words to talk to God.

Jesus, remind me daily of your constant presence in my life. Use me to accomplish your purposes and to make a difference in other people's lives. Thank you for guiding my life. Amen.

Talk With Friends

Discuss these questions in a small group:

• How have you experienced God most recently?

• Has there ever been a time in your Christian life when you were on the fence spiritually? What did you do about it?

• Describe a time God used you to make a difference (big or small) in someone's life. If nothing comes to mind, in what ways would you like God to use you in the future?

Spiritual Life

Born a Christian?

Matt's Story

I've been raised in a Christian home, and I've attended church every week since the day I was born. I made a decision at the age of five to trust Jesus as my Savior, but only because the program and teachers at Sunday school said it was a good idea to be a Christian.

As I grew up, I learned more about God, but none of what I learned seemed to apply to me. I wondered why it seemed to make so much sense to others but not to me—someone who had heard nearly every message ever spoken. (Well, it seemed like that anyway!)

It wasn't until a high school camp, when I could see no reason to keep saying I was a Christian, that I finally understood: I thought I could inherit God. I had heard preachers talking about knowing God personally, but I assumed I didn't need to know God because my parents' faith would cover me. For so long, I had thought I was just born a Christian.

> **"And without faith it is impossible to please God, because anyone who comes to him must believe that he exists and that he rewards those who earnestly seek him"** (Hebrews 11:6).

I'm not a Christian based on what my parents say and do—being a Christian is about my own personal relationship with God. My parents laid the foundation for my faith, and I'm grateful, but I had to take steps to make my faith my own.

What God Taught Me

• God wants to know everything about me: how my day was, what grades I got on an exam, what I'm feeling—everything. God desires a personal relationship with me because he loves me!

• You can begin a relationship with God by inviting him into your life.

• Reading the Bible each day changes my heart.

Write Your Story

When you have a personal relationship with someone, you want to get to know that person and spend time with him or her. In the same way, God desires to know you. Take some time to write a letter to God. Tell him about the victories and struggles you faced this week.

Dear God, this week, I...

Talk to God

Use this prayer, or use your own words to talk to God.

Jesus, I want to know you and learn more about you. Teach me about your character and how I can be more like you. Help me make my faith in you my own, not because my family believes, but because I do. Amen.

Talk With Friends

Discuss these questions in a small group:

• What's the difference between having a personal relationship with someone and just knowing about someone?

• Do you have a personal relationship with Jesus, or do you just know about him? When did the relationship start, or what's preventing you from having a relationship with him?

• Do your parents have a relationship with Jesus? If so, what influence has that had on your life so far? What are some of the advantages of growing up in a Christian home? difficulties?

Reaching Out

Michael's Story

It all started at the beginning of high school, when Jason and I were in history class together. We didn't really know each other at the beginning, but through this class we became friends.

We sat next to each other, and one day I started to share with Jason what I know about God. It was great to see how open Jason was to what I had to say, and I thank God for that. I could sense that Jason was searching for something greater than himself to fill a place in his heart that he had been trying to fill all his life. He's a major ski competitor, and he has achieved much success on the slopes, but even that couldn't fill his heart with constant peace and joy. I found out he was into Ouija boards and contact with the evil spiritual world. This didn't give him what he was looking for either.

I shared my faith with Jason and also invited him to my student ministry. A few of the leaders in my student ministry helped Jason learn about God. He eventually trusted Jesus with his life.

Jason's still skiing in races, and his life has really changed. As I'm writing this story, he's in Austria representing Australia in the Junior World Cup. Praise God that he can be a witness for Jesus when he skis! God made me see how he can totally change a life.

I knew that Jason's mom and dad needed to hear about God's truth too. My mom made an effort to get to know Jason's mom and invited her to church. A few weeks later, Jason's mom committed her heart to Jesus, which was exciting for all of us, especially Jason.

"But in your hearts set apart Christ as Lord. Always be prepared to give an answer to everyone who asks you to give the reason for the hope that you have. But do this with gentleness and respect, keeping a clear conscience, so that those who speak maliciously against your good behavior in Christ may be ashamed of their slander" (1 Peter 3:15-16).

Jason's parents have decided to split up, which is very difficult for him to deal with. His dad isn't at home anymore, and Jason lives with his mom. The next challenge is to start sharing Jesus with Jason's dad. Jason and I need to be patient and talk with him when the time is right.

What God Taught Me

• God taught me to not be ashamed to share my faith and to stand up for Jesus every chance I get.

• I learned that I'm not alone. God is watching every step I take, and he'll give me opportunities to be bold with my faith.

• I need to keep praying and trusting God and look for the doors he opens.

• God can use *me* to make a difference in someone's life!

Write Your Story

Suppose that one Monday morning a friend asks you at school, "Why did you go to church yesterday? Why is God so important in your life?" What would you say?

Talk to God

Use this prayer, or use your own words to talk to God.

Jesus, thank you for the opportunities you give me to talk about you with non-Christian family members and friends. Please give me the courage and the boldness to not let those opportunities pass by. Help me take a stand for you and talk with others about your amazing grace. Amen.

Talk With Friends

Discuss these questions in a small group:

• At school, how easy is it to tell who is a Christian and who isn't? What are some of the ways you can tell the difference? Would your classmates know where you stand? Why?

Read Colossians 4:5-6 together: "Be wise in the way you act toward out-siders [non-Christians]; make the most of every opportunity. Let your conversation be always full of grace, seasoned with salt, so that you may know how to answer everyone."

• How confident are you in sharing the story of your spiritual journey with others? What could help you be bolder with your faith?

• Who would you like to share the love of Christ with? After everyone has shared a name, take time to pray as a group for those people.

Praying for a Miracle
Kathy's Story

In seventh grade, I was diagnosed with lupus, a chronic autoimmune disease. To help treat the damage to my kidneys, the doctors decided to give me a series of treatments similar to chemotherapy. I started these monthly treatments the summer before my sophomore year of high school. After a year, the frequency of the doses was reduced to once every three months. After two and a half years of missing Fridays at school and weekends of fun, I was finally finished in November of my senior year. I was so happy not to have to deal with the nausea anymore and to give my red hair a chance to grow. (I never went bald, but I did lose a lot of hair.)

Five months after I finished my treatments, my test results began to reflect a decline in the health of my kidneys. During one of my routine doctor appointments, I was told that I might have to return to the nauseating, hair-stealing treatments. I was devastated! With college just around the corner, the last thing I wanted to deal with was more time-consuming, stomach-turning trips to the hospital.

I immediately began to pray. I knew that God had a plan for me and if I trusted in that plan, his peace would get me through, however the situation turned out. I gave my situation to God through prayer and let him take care of it because I knew there was nothing I could do. I also talked to my Christian friends and student ministry leaders and asked them to pray for me.

Never before had I devoted myself to praying for one thing. Every time my situation crossed my mind, I lifted it up to God. In my prayers, I told God how I felt, and I just asked that his will would be done. If I needed the treatments to improve my health, then that was fine. I trusted that God had the best in store for my life.

A few weeks after the test results had shown a decline in my health and I had begun to pray, I went back to the doctor. More tests were done, and later I went in for the results.

> **"Cast all your anxiety on him because he cares for you" (1 Peter 5:7).**

It was amazing! My kidney function was close to normal, and a lot of the other test results showed great improvement. The doctor decided there was no need for more treatments. I know the good news was a gift from God.

There was absolutely no earthly or medical reason for my test results to have improved that much in such a short period of time. I'm convinced it was because of prayer and the power of God.

What God Taught Me

• The biggest lesson God taught me was the tremendous power of prayer. Prayer can change a life—I know it changed mine!

• God also taught me the value of good Christian friends. Being able to go to my friends with prayer requests was an awesome thing. I felt comforted and secure knowing my friends were praying for me.

• I learned not only to pray and tell God what I wanted, but also to trust him with my life. When I prayed, God knew how I felt, but he also knew that I completely believed that whatever he wanted for me was the best thing for my life.

• In his perfect timing and way, God answers every request I bring before him.

Write Your Story

It's easy to be distracted while praying. A useful discipline is to write your prayers to God. You can phrase them in the form of a letter. Use the space below to write a prayer. Make sure to take time to thank God for the work he is doing in your life. Try not to pray only about difficulties or struggles you're facing, but also tell God about your victories and thank him for his faithfulness. Later, read what you wrote here. It will be awesome to see how God has answered your prayers.

Dear God...

Talk to God

Use this prayer, or use your own words to talk to God.

Jesus, I know you're faithful. You've proven that to me time after time. Thank you for the many ways you bless my life with good things. Help me trust you when times are tough and I feel alone. I know you'll walk with me every step of the way. Amen.

Talk With Friends

Discuss these questions in a small group:

• Talk about a time God answered your prayers.

• If you pray regularly, what do you most often talk to God about?

• What can we do as a group to help one another be more committed to praying?

Standing on the Word
Ryan's Story

Last year, one of my close friends died in a tragic car accident. The tragedy shook everyone at school and made us realize that life is short. Many students asked questions like "Could that really happen to me?" and "What happens after you die?" Some of my friends had questions about spiritual matters, especially heaven and hell.

I was guilt-stricken as I asked myself why I had never taken the time to talk to my friend about God. I won't know if he knew God personally until I get to heaven. I was disappointed in myself for not being bold with my faith and for missing the opportunities God had given me. I wanted so badly to turn the clock back just so I could have a chance to talk with him again.

> **"The grass withers and the flowers fall, but the word of our God stands forever" (Isaiah 40:8).**

Unfortunately, it sometimes takes a tragedy to change one's life. Soon after my friend died, I started talking to my other friends at school about God. I asked them about their ideas and beliefs, and they responded with unpredictable and unanswerable questions. I learned very quickly that without God's Word in my heart and without the guidance of the Holy Spirit through prayer, I was virtually useless. I knew I had to be better equipped with the Word of God.

What God Taught Me

• God taught me about the power of his Word, the Bible. I started reading the Bible daily, memorizing key verses that I could use to share my faith.

• Testimonies about what God has done and is doing in my life are a great way to encourage and challenge friends. They prove that God is real and is interested in participating in our lives.

• I can be bold and confident with my non-Christian friends. They need to hear that God can radically change their lives and that they matter to him.

Write Your Story

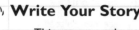

This story may have reminded you that our life on earth is short, especially compared to eternity in heaven. Ask God to give you an opportunity to talk about him with a friend this week.

Talk to God

Use this prayer, or use your own words to talk to God.

Jesus, please give me compassion for my friends who don't know you. I want to share my faith and to tell my friends of your loving grace. I pray that I may go to school and watch lives change through the work you'll do there. Amen.

Talk With Friends

Discuss these questions in a small group:

• What's your favorite book of the Bible? your favorite Bible story or verse? Why?

• What has helped you learn more about God's Word? How often do you read the Bible?

• What hinders you from telling your friends about Jesus?

Speaking Up

Chris' Story

During my sophomore year, I was in a journalism class. Almost every student in the class knew I was a Christian, but I never went out of my way to talk about my faith. During class, we usually discussed current issues facing society. Topics would often come up about which I had particular feelings because of my Christian faith, but I tried to keep my opinions to myself.

One day, a topic came up that I had a hard time keeping quiet about. The class started talking about morals, spirituality, and faith in God. I sat there amazed and extremely hurt by what many of my classmates were saying about my faith, but I wasn't sure if I was ready to take on a class that was entirely against me. I thought to myself, "If I keep my mouth shut, no one will know my opinion and I can quietly walk out of class." Well, that idea wasn't part of God's plan!

I turned to a friend sitting next to me and said, "Boy, am I biting my tongue!"

She responded, "Why don't you say something? Don't just sit here. I want to hear what you have to say." Then many of my classmates and my teacher directed the intense discussion at me. My teacher asked for my opinion. I was torn. I wasn't sure what to say.

I took a moment to pray for God's direction. I thought, "If I don't say something, my friends won't get the chance to hear about Jesus." So I decided to voice my beliefs.

> **"Don't let anyone look down on you because you are young, but set an example for the believers in speech, in life, in love, in faith and in purity"** (1 Timothy 4:12).

I began by saying that I believe in God, love attending church, and spend time with God every day...all of this by my free will. Then I was able to explain what I believe the Bible says about the topic at hand.

I even went on to tell my friends how they, too, could trust Jesus and begin a personal relationship with him. I was amazed at how each person listened to me, and at the end, some had questions for me about my faith. It was awesome!

I walked out of my journalism class that day thankful that God had challenged me to speak up. To my knowledge, no one became a Christian that day, but I know God used me to plant seeds in my classmates' hearts.

What God Taught Me

- When I'm open and available, God can use me to make a difference.
- God is always with me, and I can pray throughout my day.
- God guides me and gives me the right words to say. All I need is a willing heart.

Write Your Story

If I ever get the chance to talk about God in one of my classes, this is what I'll say...

Talk to God

Use this prayer, or use your own words to talk to God.

Jesus, you're so amazing. You've done so much in my life and changed my heart in many different ways. I want my friends to know you and to begin to understand the difference you can make in their lives. Please give me the boldness to speak about you whenever opportunities come my way. Amen.

Talk With Friends

Discuss these questions in a small group:

• On a scale of one (for sure) to ten (no way), how likely would you be to stand up for God in one of your classes? Why?

• If a friend asked you, "Why is your life different?" or "Why are you involved at church?" what would you say?

• Take a minute to tell your story: What was your life like before you met God? What is your life like now? What do you think the future holds?

A Grateful Heart

Julie's Story

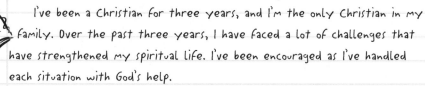

I've been a Christian for three years, and I'm the only Christian in my family. Over the past three years, I have faced a lot of challenges that have strengthened my spiritual life. I've been encouraged as I've handled each situation with God's help.

Now I'm in the middle of overcoming more obstacles: For the last four months, my parents have been fighting, and my dad has been threatening to leave us. School is tough, and I've been getting in a lot of trouble. I've been failing most of my exams. I feel alone; I have no one to talk to. My friends always seem too busy, and when I've prayed, I've felt as if no one was listening—as if God doesn't care about what's happening in my life. I have felt empty when I prayed, even though I seem to need God the most when I'm in these difficult situations.

> **"You will seek me and find me when you seek me with all your heart" (Jeremiah 29:13).**

But recently I decided to change the way I pray. Instead of telling God all my problems, I have started telling him that he's awesome and thanking him for all the good things in my life I can think of. I've started to worship God, even though I don't always feel like it.

Since I've been praising God like this, something has happened in my spirit, and I've gained a new perspective. Instead of focusing on all the hard things in my life, I've begun to focus on the many ways God blesses me each day.

What God Taught Me

- Some times are hard for a reason. These challenges have strengthened my character and have taught me how to persevere when things are rough. With each challenge, God gives me a chance to grow and learn.
- God loves me so much. I'm precious to him.
- God cares about my every need and can meet all of those needs.
- I can trust God, knowing he has a perfect plan for my life.

Write Your Story

It's pretty cool to remember that God watches over us and finds joy in meeting our needs. Psalm 23 compares God to a shepherd. Consider the different ways he's with us and cares for us:

"The Lord is my shepherd, I shall not be in want. He makes me lie down in green pastures, he leads me beside quiet waters, he restores my soul. He guides me in paths of righteousness for his name's sake. Even though I walk through the valley of the shadow of death, I will fear no evil, for you are with me; your rod and your staff, they comfort me. You prepare a table before me in the presence of my enemies. You anoint my head with oil; my cup overflows. Surely goodness and love will follow me all the days of my life, and I will dwell in the house of the Lord forever."

What comfort does this Scripture passage give you?

Talk to God

Use this prayer, or use your own words to talk to God.

Jesus, you're a giver of good gifts. Remind me of your goodness and the many ways you bless my life. Help me to remember your blessings and to thank you for all you give me. Amen.

Talk With Friends

Discuss these questions in a small group:

• What was the last gift you received? Who was it from, and how did you respond: with a thank-you note? a phone call? no response?

• How do you express your thankfulness to God?

• What do you need from God the Shepherd today: guidance? comfort? a sense of security? peace? rest? protection? Explain your answer.

Life on the Edge
Mark's Story

I've often wondered what heaven and hell are like. I've been curious, but I never imagined that I would experience a living hell.

I grew up going to church, and I had a little knowledge of God and the Bible. But I allowed the Evil One to pull me into the ways of the world, and I learned to live in his deceptions. It started with subtle, small things. I began to reason with myself that wrong things were right. Before I knew it, I went from being a respectful and honest young man to being a disrespectful and unruly guy. Each day I pushed the boundaries a bit further until I was living a life without any boundaries.

Drinking, smoking, and cursing became the norm in my life. Sex was a regular occurrence. As crazy as it sounds, I even kept charts of my sexual conquests and had a point system. But I was never satisfied. I was in and out of the juvenile office. I thought everything was cool until, one day, I looked around and saw what a dark life I was living.

Each time I did something destructive, I felt pain, and my life became even darker. But it wasn't enough to stop me. I continued to do harmful and sinful things. I felt that I couldn't break out of the vicious cycle. I became angry and started to fight. I had lots of offers from girls. I was known as the life of the party, but no one knew about the battle that was raging inside me. Eventually, my behavior got me kicked out of school. But changing schools didn't change my lifestyle and destructive habits.

Thankfully, though, God didn't give up on me. One summer weekend, I went to a youth retreat sponsored by the church my family attended. Me, of all people! I went only because I wanted to check out the hot girls who might be there and see if I could add them to my conquest chart. Instead of seeing the pretty girls, I saw the worst sight in my entire life. I saw the real me. It wasn't a pretty picture.

I saw the destruction and felt the pain my lifestyle choices had wreaked on my body and spirit. I broke down and cried. I kept thinking about all the bad choices I had made in my life. Have you ever cried over seeing the real you? God's light and holiness began to highlight each sin I had ever committed. It was a difficult process, but one I'm grateful to have gone through.

> **"If you confess with your mouth, 'Jesus is Lord,' and believe in your heart that God raised him from the dead, you will be saved"** (Romans 10:9).

After much reflection, I decided to commit my life to God and to turn my life around. I asked God to forgive me and to give me a clean slate through Jesus' death on the cross for my sins.

What God Taught Me

- God rescued me before it was too late. He gave me a clean slate.
- God never gave up on me.
- God will never let me go or leave me. Even when I'm tempted or rebellious, God will never walk away.

Write Your Story

Think of a time you've been tempted to walk away from God. Thank God for not giving up on you.

Talk to God

Use this prayer, or use your own words to talk to God.

Jesus, you're full of grace and mercy. Thank you for continuing to rescue me and pull me out of danger. I know that you're a holy God and that my sins have consequences and deserve punishment. Thank you for taking the punishment for me and for dying on the cross for my sins. Amen.

Talk With Friends

Discuss these questions in a small group:

• What do you think happens when a person dies? What do you think will happen to you?

• Movies, books, and music portray heaven and hell in different ways. What do you think heaven will look and feel like? What about hell? What does the Bible have to say about heaven and hell?

• Has there ever been a time of rebellion in your life? What influenced you to act that way?

Staying on the Path
Brittany's Story

The summer before high school, I sang a song at my church that really influenced my life. The song was about not wanting to live a casual and lukewarm Christian life. I made a commitment that summer to show all my friends, my teachers, and anyone else I met during high school that I was a Christian. Being a Christian was more than just a name I wanted to call my-self. I wanted my actions to prove it.

It hasn't been an easy road. The ways of the world can be pretty pow-erful and enticing. I've had to make some hard choices to live a truly Christ-ian lifestyle. For example, I attend very few parties where alcohol or drugs are abundant. If I do go to a party where that stuff is present, no one could ever say they saw me with a beer or a joint. I'm thankful I've stayed strong, but it has been a battle. Whenever I find myself at the end of a tough battle, I'm reminded of how much more satisfying God is than the "fun" things of this world. God gives me an inner peace that no amount of beer or drugs ever could.

I'll be honest, though. At times I've wondered if it's really worth it to stay on God's path. At one point I was fed up and wanted to have just a little part of what the world had to offer. I thought I could take my chances and get wasted once in my life. Why not just once?

But just as I was ready to take a break from my Christian lifestyle, God hit me with a harsh reality. A friend of mine was killed in a car accident. This guy lived an awesome life for God. He led a truly Christian life that couldn't be disputed. It was at his funeral that I asked myself how I would want to be remembered if I were to die. How would I want my family and friends to remember me?

I decided I wanted to be remembered as a woman who followed God, not as a silly schoolgirl who got drunk on Saturday nights and showed up for church on Sunday mornings. I want people to see the one thing that means the most to me, and that's my relationship with God. If I want to live a Christian life, that means following God's plan for my life.

> **"Your word is a lamp to my feet and a light for my path" (Psalm 119:105).**

My friends have noticed. They see something different about me, and they wonder why I don't do the things they do. They've observed that I've chosen not to drink or have sex, and they ask me why. Living this way has initiated many conversations about my faith. People are watching, and I've tried my best to be an example for God.

What God Taught Me

• Through the Bible, God has taught me about the kinds of things that please him and how I can make good choices with his help.

• God helped me determine my boundaries and convictions.

• People notice how I live my life. When I try to live a life of Christian integrity, others can see that something about me is different.

• Being involved in the student ministry at my church is awesome. I am surrounded by friends who encourage me to keep making the right choices and to not live a casual Christian life. It's also a great place to bring my non-Christian friends and introduce them to God.

Write Your Story

How can you prevent yourself from becoming a casual Christian? What can you do to empower yourself to make good choices? Write a few steps you can take, and ask God to provide you with the strength to live a life fully devoted to him.

Talk to God

Use this prayer, or use your own words to talk to God.

Jesus, I don't want to be a casual Christian. Help me fight the temptations of this world and walk with you. Remind me that others see my actions and that I may affect their lives by what I do. I want my life to glorify you. Please help me live in such a way that others see your work in me. Amen.

Talk With Friends

Discuss these questions in a small group:

• Has anyone ever noticed something different about you because of your relationship with God? Do your speech and actions stand apart from the crowd?

• How can you be more intentional in sharing your faith with your friends?

In Revelation 3:15-16, God talks about being a lukewarm Christian: "I know your deeds, that you are neither cold nor hot. I wish you were either one or the other! So, because you are lukewarm—neither hot nor cold—I am about to spit you out of my mouth."

   • In what areas of your life do you feel lukewarm? In what areas does your faith need to heat up?

Home Life

If Only

Eric's Story

Relatives weren't exactly my favorite people to hang around with, but I could tolerate them for a few hours every once in a while. I never saw them as people who needed Jesus until my uncle died. I regretted the time I could have spent with him, knowing I could have shared my faith with him.

When my mother first told me that her brother had drunk himself to death, I sat in shocked silence. Inside my head I screamed, "How could this have happened?" My aunt was the one expected to die; she was the one with cancer, the one who knew Jesus as her Savior. Nothing had prepared me for the upsetting news. All the signs from my uncle's life, especially his rejection of Christ, indicated he was far from heaven's door.

Guilt and grief wracked my heart following his death. I had barely talked about the weather with this man, so Christianity was not a familiar topic of conversation between us. I felt anger toward God for taking my uncle before he knew Christ, and I felt guilt for not having tried harder to reach him with the love of God. In the back of my mind, I knew God has a reason for everything, but on the surface I felt only grief and bitterness.

> **"Surely he took up our infirmities and carried our sorrows" (Isaiah 53:4a).**

I questioned God when he allowed my uncle to slip into death without knowing Christ. I asked God for answers and prayed that my uncle had become a Christian on his last day, but I knew the chances of this were slim.

What God Taught Me

• Through prayer and the Bible, I learned that God won't always make the pain go away, but he'll always be there to offer peace. I found that his constant presence was the best healing I could ever receive.

• In those silent times, when it seemed as if God had no answer, I know now that he was there beside me.

• God used this situation for his good, shaking me from my casual Christian lifestyle and showing me that I'll have to step out of my comfort zone to share my faith. God woke me up and opened my eyes to the many people in my every-day life who need to hear about him. My uncle's death pushed me to be bolder in talking about my faith.

Write Your Story

Take time today to think about your friends and family members who don't yet have a personal relationship with Jesus Christ. Use the space below to write their names as a reminder to pray for opportunities to share your faith with them.

Talk to God

Use this prayer, or use your own words to talk to God.

Jesus, I want the world to know about your amazing grace! Give me new eyes and compassion to see the family members and friends around me who don't yet know you. Use me to point them to you. Let my speech and actions reflect you. Amen.

Talk With Friends

Discuss these questions in a small group:

• Has someone close to you ever died? If so, how did you feel? How did God help you through the situation?

• Sharing your faith with non-Christian friends and family members takes courage. Have you ever been bold with your faith? If so, explain. If not, what holds you back?

Read Isaiah 41:10 together, and encourage each other to memorize it: "So do not fear, for I am with you; do not be dismayed, for I am your God. I will strengthen you and help you; I will uphold you with my righteous right hand."

• How has God given you strength to deal with an issue you have recently faced?

Family Secrets

Ashley's Story

I was really excited when my aunt announced that her family would be moving to our town. They had lived far away from us all my life. Now I would get a chance to know my aunt, uncle, and cousins better. Six months after they moved, my uncle invited my cousins and me to go with him to a car show in our small town. It ended up that I was the only one able to go.

As we walked through the car displays, he described the old cars and what was special about each one. Then my uncle reached for my hand and held it. I was shocked, so shocked that I didn't pull away. I didn't think it would go any further, but I was wrong. He then told me he needed to check on a shop he was responsible for to see if everything was OK. Since we were nearby, we went in. During the ten to fifteen minutes we were in the shop, my uncle sexually abused me.

I didn't tell anyone about what had happened. Instead, I just stuffed it all down inside. My aunt and uncle went away for several months after that. When they returned, I was cold toward my uncle, so he asked his daughter to ask me why I was avoiding him. I told her the whole story. That gave me the courage to also tell my parents. My parents had a hard time accepting what my uncle had done to me. I had all my feelings stuffed deep down, and I hadn't realized that I wasn't to blame. I was close to suicide because the whole thing was eating away at me. I had been planning to go on a missions trip the following summer, and that was one of the few reasons I didn't commit suicide.

During that missions trip, I got some help from a professional Christian counselor and was able, with God's

> "The Lord is close to the brokenhearted and saves those who are crushed in spirit" (Psalm 34:18).

help, to work out this difficult issue and a flood of emotions. I finally began to accept my innocence in this event and began to experience forgiveness and healing.

The counselor encouraged me to write letters to the people involved, addressing how I felt and how they had hurt me. This exercise really helped me. I didn't need to send the letters; just writing them helped bring some healing.

If you've experienced similar pain in your life, God is there to take you through the healing process if you'll ask him.

What God Taught Me

• God taught me that no matter what I'm going through, he remains faithful, and that when I'm hurting, he is hurting with me.

• It's hard to forgive others, but God gives me the strength and softens my heart when forgiveness is needed.

• I've become more understanding toward people who are hurting. God has enlarged my heart and taught me about compassion.

• Just because I'm a Christian, I'm not immune to hard times. But God is with me through all the peaks and valleys.

• It's damaging to suppress feelings and carry secrets. Don't do it! Tell someone, and get professional help if you need it.

Write Your Story

Can you relate to this story, or do you know someone with a similar story? If so, write a prayer to God, asking him for emotional healing. If not, thank God for protecting you from such emotional pain.

Talk to God

Use this prayer, or use your own words to talk to God.

Jesus, you know how hard life can be. Some of the things I've experienced are very painful. Heal my wounds and show me what I need to do to become whole again. Thank you for being a powerful and faithful God. Amen.

Talk With Friends

Discuss these questions in a small group:

• When have you had to forgive someone who wronged you? What did you do or say?

• How was God faithful in carrying you through a trial?

• What would you tell a friend who has been sexually abused? Would you tell him or her to seek to offer forgiveness? find help? tell someone? What encouragement and advice would you give?

When the Storms Hit Home
Brett's Story

I became a Christian at the age of six and went to church my whole life. Being raised in a Christian home has laid a strong foundation for my life, and I'm grateful for my upbringing.

My dad has had a very rough life. Before I was born, he had a kidney transplant that lasted twenty-one years. A few years ago, the kidney started to fail him. He was put on a dialysis machine for many months. During this time, he was always tired or sick because of the medicine he was taking. I knew my dad needed a new kidney to feel better.

My uncle turned out to be a perfect match, and he gave one of his kidneys to my dad (his brother). Since this second transplant, my dad has had knee surgery, rotator cuff surgery, colon cancer, and a tumor on his spine. Many times

> "I have told you these things, so that in me you may have peace. In this world you will have trouble. But take heart! I have overcome the world" (John 16:33).

doctors have told us that a surgery might not work or that my dad might not survive. Most days he doesn't feel well.

It's been hard to have a dad who is sick so often. I sometimes miss all the things a lot of fathers can do with their sons, but I'm thankful that my dad is alive and such an important part of my life.

What God Taught Me

- God has never failed me or let me down. He's been faithful to my family and me.

- I've grown stronger in my faith through all my dad's health problems. I've learned about the power of prayer and how much God loves me.

- Without God, I have no idea where I would be. When I think about my life and all I've faced, I see that God has given me many blessings.

- If I want to live as Jesus did, I need to read about him and get to know who he really is, so I've started to read the Bible. It's awesome to learn about how Jesus lived so I can try to pattern my life after his.

Write Your Story

Read Psalm 121. Write down what this passage says about God's faithfulness when hard times come your way. Thank God for these promises.

Talk to God

Use this prayer, or use your own words to talk to God.

Jesus, sometimes life is hard. I always seem to be facing some kind of challenge. Thank you for being by my side and giving me the strength to face every situation. You're my rock and my safe place when times are difficult. I praise you for your faithfulness. Amen.

Talk With Friends

Discuss these questions in a small group:

• What do you do when you're anxious or dealing with tough issues? Do you eat? withdraw to your room? bite your nails? pray?

• When you're facing a challenge, who do you turn to for support, strength, and help? Why?

• Has anyone close to you ever had a serious health problem? How did you deal with it?

Choosing to Forgive
Megan's Story

"Why would you want to eat that? You're already fat. Everyone who looks at you notices how big you are."

"You are so annoying. I can't stand you when you're like that."

"You're such a spoiled brat, and sometimes I think you're neurotic. Are all girls your age so neurotic?"

"I'm the one who has lived in this house with you and watched you grow up. Your father has never lived under the same roof as you, so he doesn't know what you're really like. If he really knew you the way I do, I'm sure he wouldn't like you either."

> "You have heard that it was said, 'Love your neighbor and hate your enemy.' But I tell you: Love your enemies and pray for those who persecute you, that you may be sons of your Father in heaven" (Matthew 5:43-45a).

You're fat, you're annoying. If people are told these things often enough, they start to believe them. My stepfather has been saying these kinds of things to me for fifteen years. Not every day has been horrible. I have some good memories, but somehow those good times can't overcome all the hurt and anger I've felt for so long.

For years, I've covered up my pain by hiding it,

burying it, and pretending I wasn't deeply hurt by my stepfather's words. It wasn't until very recently that I decided it was OK to feel frustrated and angry and to be authentic with my feelings. Through many months of praying and asking other people to pray for me, I'm working toward complete forgiveness of my stepfather.

What God Taught Me

• God is the ultimate forgiver and has taught me a lot about forgiveness—not just the meaning of the word, but the action required to fulfill its definition. I had to turn to God and realize that he has forgiven me thousands of times. If God can forgive me, I need to forgive my stepfather.

• Forgiveness doesn't mean I'll never hurt again or that I'll be immune to more pain. Forgiveness is a choice that requires God's help in preparing my heart.

• Prayer helps me recognize the pain I'm feeling. I can ask God to help me understand my feelings.

• One of the difficult steps in the forgiveness process is confronting the person who has hurt me. Matthew 18:15-20 is our model for confronting people in truth and love.

Write Your Story

Is there someone you need to forgive? Take time to write a letter to God. Ask for wisdom and courage in dealing with your situation. Reflect on the person you need to forgive, and make a commitment to act. If no one comes to mind, is there anyone you have wronged and whose forgiveness you need to seek?

Talk to God

Use this prayer, or use your own words to talk to God.

Jesus, sometimes it's hard to forgive the people who have hurt me. It would be so much easier to be mean in return or to seek revenge. Teach me how to forgive others just as you have forgiven me. Thank you for giving me second chances and for loving me. Amen.

Talk With Friends

Discuss these questions in a small group:

• What does it mean to be forgiven by God?

• When was the last time someone close to you hurt you? How did you react?

• When was the last time you showed forgiveness to someone? Was it hard for you to do? What steps did you take?

Amazing Grace
Jennifer's Story

I'll remember a night in December for the rest of my life. Christmas, my favorite holiday, was right around the corner. I was completely content with my life. Then, in one night, my life was turned upside down.

My older brother called late at night to tell us that he and my mom had been in a car accident. My dad, my younger brother, and I rushed to the scene as horrible thoughts raced through my mind. By the time we arrived and saw the ruined car, I was sick with panic, which only intensified when I learned that my mom had been airlifted to the hospital. We left the scene and sped to the hospital.

After sitting nervously in the waiting room for what seemed like an eternity, the doctor informed us that my mom would remain in the hospital for the next three or four months.

My older brother was fine, but it would be days before we knew the extent of my mom's injuries. I was in a trance, not knowing exactly what was going on. My family tried to protect me from knowing just how bad things were. It wasn't until the first time I was allowed to see my mom that I realized that she might never be the same again.

My mom underwent two extensive surgeries and remained in the hospital for a month. I truly believe several miracles occurred during that time. The surgeries were completed without any complications, even though at first she wasn't expected to live. She returned home but still had a long recovery ahead of her.

> **"And we know that in all things God works for the good of those who love him, who have been called according to his purpose"** **(Romans 8:28).**

The doctors predicted that my mom might never walk again. She went through months of physical therapy. Through faith and determination, she built up enough strength to prove them wrong. Even though life isn't as easy for her as it once was, God didn't take her away from us. I'll never stop being grateful for that.

What God Taught Me

• God taught me about the power of prayer. I know that many people prayed for my mom every day.

• God never left my family all alone to struggle with this situation. The people from our church did everything possible to help us. They prayed for us, cooked meals for us, and offered their time. I was able to see the beauty of God's church in action as people reached out to my family.

• It's important to be grateful for the little things, like the fact that my mom is alive today and can give me a hug in the morning.

• God is constantly working things out according to his plan for my life.

• I've learned to look not only for extraordinary miracles, but also for the small miracles God works every day.

Write Your Story

It's easy to forget about the goodness of God. He's a generous and gracious God who loves to give gifts to his children! What can you thank God for today?

Talk to God

Use this prayer, or use your own words to talk to God.

Jesus, you regularly give me good gifts and bless my life in countless ways. Forgive me for taking these gifts for granted and not thanking you for them. Teach me to see your goodness each day. Amen.

Talk With Friends

Discuss these questions in a small group:

• What are three things you're thankful for? Do you ever take these things for granted?

Read 1 Peter 5:7 together: "Cast all your anxiety on him because he cares for you."

• Are you anxious and worried about anything right now? How can you turn the situation over to God?

• What small miracles has God done for you?

Phantom Father
Dan's Story

Have you ever wondered what it would be like to wake up in the morning to the sight of your dad in the kitchen with a cup of coffee in his hand? I have. Have you ever played a sport and looked into the bleachers to find your mom smiling and clapping by herself? I have. Have you ever watched your mom struggle to work, pay the bills, and take care of you? I have.

I've asked God again and again why I've never met my father and why he isn't involved in my life. Why would God allow me to be raised without a father figure in my home? Why would God allow my mom to raise two children all by herself? Why don't I even know what my dad looks like?

For years I've struggled with feelings of abandonment and being unwanted. I used to pray every night that God would let me see my father just once. But so far, God hasn't granted me that request. As I've grown in my faith, I don't question God as much. I know he has a great plan for my life and for my family. I've learned to trust him fully.

> "How great is the love the Father has lavished on us, that we should be called children of God! And that is what we are! The reason the world does not know us is that it did not know him" (1 John 3:1).

What God Taught Me

• Growing up without a dad has been a big, difficult, sad part of my life. But God has provided other influential males from my church who have walked with me along the way.

• God has erased my feelings of rejection and emptiness and replaced them with feelings of being unconditionally loved by him, my perfect heavenly Father.

• I can give my problems to Jesus. He knows everything I've gone through and has promised to never leave my side.

• While my earthly father has disappointed me, my Father in heaven will never forsake me or let me down.

Write Your Story

Give thanks to God for your earthly father, then thank God for being your heavenly Father.

Talk to God

Use this prayer, or use your own words to talk to God.

Jesus, thank you for being faithful to me. I praise you for your goodness, kindness, love, and grace. Thank you for being an example to me of a perfect Father. Please heal my heart of any sadness regarding my earthly father, and give me a sense of peace and joy that can come only from you. Amen.

Talk With Friends

Discuss these questions in a small group:

• How would you describe your relationship with your father?

• What is a favorite memory you have with your mom or dad?

• How can this small group pray for you regarding your family?

 # Social Life

Taking a Stand

Nicole's Story

One day as I was walking outside my school, I noticed one of the girls in my freshman class sitting on the ground crying. Her name was Whitney, and she had the reputation of being a bit wild (attending all the parties and smoking in the bathrooms between classes). I'd never had much to do with her up until that moment, and I didn't know what she would think of me. I asked her what was wrong. I sat down next to her as she told me her story.

It had happened on New Year's Eve. She had been at a party with friends, and lots of alcohol and drugs were available. She had drunk too much and had lost consciousness. She had ended up having sex with a seventeen-year-old guy. (We were thirteen at the time.) She woke up the next morning beside this guy she didn't even know.

She told me more. A few weeks after that disastrous party, she found out she was pregnant. She planned to have an abortion, but she miscarried instead. Her best friend was the only other person who knew about the situation but one day decided to tell a few people about it. The students began calling Whitney names and labeling her "easy."

I just hugged her and let her cry as I silently prayed for wisdom and the right words to say to her. I gave her my phone number so she could call me anytime she needed to talk. The bell rang, and we went inside to class.

Over the next few days, I couldn't get her off my mind, and I kept praying for her. I had a chance to talk further with her, and I told her about God. She told me she found it hard to believe God existed after all she had experienced.

My heart broke for her, and one night I wrote her a four-page letter that explained that God loved her, that he had a purpose and plan for her life, and that she didn't need sex or alcohol to fill her empty heart. I described how she could have a relationship with God and receive forgiveness for her past mistakes.

The next day, I was so nervous about giving her the letter because I knew that as soon as I gave it to her, there was no taking it back. I handed it to her in class, and she read it right away. By the next day, almost everyone in the whole school had heard about it. All my friends thought I was some kind of psycho, and they deserted me. Over night I had gone from having plenty of friends to having none. It seemed like a disaster. But now that everyone knew I was living for Jesus, I decided to live and lead by example and not to be a hypocrite.

It was tough to feel abandoned by my friends, but God never left me. He gave me opportunities to talk about him that I wouldn't have had before. In different classes, people asked me spiritual questions, sometimes sarcastic, sometimes not. My classmates began to see that my actions lined up with my words. Slowly they began to respect me. I finally found a new group of friends and have had the chance to talk about God with them. Two of them have given their lives to God.

"Whoever acknowledges me before men, I will also acknowledge him before my Father in heaven. But whoever disowns me before men, I will disown him before my Father in heaven" (Matthew 10:32-33).

After I gave Whitney the letter, she hated me and wouldn't speak to me for months. That hurt me, and I didn't understand it, but gradually we became friends. She respects my beliefs and always asks me for advice. I know that she'll never find true healing or release from her problems until she gives her life to Jesus. I'll continue to pray for her.

What God Taught Me

• No matter how hard it is at times, I have to take a stand for God.

• Risks are worth taking when someone's eternity is at stake.

• My actions are more important than my words. If my actions hadn't lined up with my words, my friends would have considered me a hypocrite.

• It's important to read the Bible and pray every day. God's Word gave me confidence by showing me answers to most of the questions my classmates threw at me. Prayer kept me connected to God and gave me strength.

• Serving God is my top priority, and I'll continue to live for him each day.

Write Your Story

Who do you need to reach out to? Write a prayer asking God to help you show his love to your friends and family that do not know him.

Talk to God

Use this prayer, or use your own words to talk to God.

Jesus, give me the courage to stand up for you. I pray that I won't be shy in sharing my faith with others, but that instead I'll stand up for you with confidence. Prepare me today to share my faith in you. I want others to know what a difference you've made in my life. Amen.

Talk With Friends

Discuss these questions in a small group:

• Have you ever been rejected by someone for talking about your faith? How did you feel?

• When have you compromised your beliefs? How did you feel?

• Who among your friends could you pray for, asking God to give you the courage to share your faith with them?

Drawing the Line
Kelly's Story

I dated Jeff for four and a half months. We are both Christians, and he is really nice, so I thought it would be a good relationship. But over the course of those months, we went further physically than we should have. We're both still virgins and are incredibly grateful for that. However, during those months, every time we did something we shouldn't have, I had mixed emotions. First I would think, "We really shouldn't be doing this. It's not what God wants," but then I would think that everything was all right because Jeff and I loved each other. I came to realize how easily I could be deceived in tempting situations. I tried to talk to Jeff about it, but he didn't understand where I was coming from. He couldn't see why I didn't want to go so far even though I loved him. He would get mad, and I would give in.

> "Trust in the Lord with all your heart and lean not on your own understanding; in all your ways acknowledge him, and he will make your paths straight" (Proverbs 3:5-6).

Finally, I wasn't sure if I loved him. I prayed about it a lot. It still wasn't clear to me whether God wanted me to break up with him. It's hard to see or hear the truth when your emotions are out of control.

Four days after I completely gave my situation to God, the solution became clear. At a big youth event at church, I kept praying, asking God for wisdom. He showed me that my next step should be to break up with Jeff. I broke up with Jeff later that night, and nothing has ever felt so right.

What God Taught Me

• God cares about all areas of my life.

• I had to ask God for forgiveness and grace. The next, and harder, step was to forgive myself. I still feel bad about what I did with Jeff, but God is awesome! He used the situation for good. Since then, I've been able to talk to my best friend, who recently became a Christian, about what God has taught me.

• I learned to set boundaries when I'm dating. For example, I've decided I won't do more than kiss, I won't be alone with a guy in tempting situations, and I'll make sure the other person has the same boundaries as I do.

• God will give me the strength to overcome any temptation I face.

Write Your Story

Do you have personal convictions about how far you'll go in a dating relationship? Have you set boundaries in this area? What do you think God would want your convictions and boundaries to be in a dating relationship? Talk to him about it here.

Talk to God

Use this prayer, or use your own words to talk to God.

Jesus, I want to remain sexually pure until I am married. Strengthen my convictions. Help me set and keep the right boundaries for my dating relationships. Amen.

Talk With Friends

Discuss these questions in a small group:

• What's your idea of the perfect date?

• Have you set any boundaries for dating relationships? If so, how did you decide what they should be? If not, what do you think God would want you to do?

• Why is it important to set standards for yourself, especially before you find yourself in difficult situations? Why is it important to tell the person you're dating about your standards?

Real Friends

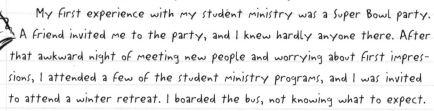

Taylor's Story

My first experience with my student ministry was a Super Bowl party. A friend invited me to the party, and I knew hardly anyone there. After that awkward night of meeting new people and worrying about first impressions, I attended a few of the student ministry programs, and I was invited to attend a winter retreat. I boarded the bus, not knowing what to expect.

The minute I stepped on the bus, I was accepted as if I were a regular. Everyone was kind and took an interest in me. I was amazed when I realized I had made more friends that weekend than I had in my whole life up to that point. I had formed authentic friendships, unlike the cliques and games I was used to with other friends. My new friends lived and treated each other differently. They had a certain joy and peace I had never seen before. I wanted what they had.

> "Two are better than one, because they have a good return for their work: If one falls down, his friend can help him up. But pity the man who falls and has no one to help him up!" (Ecclesiastes 4:9, 10).

What they had turned out to be a personal relationship with Jesus Christ. As a result of teaching I received and conversations during that weekend, I made a decision to commit my life to Christ. It was the best decision I've ever made.

What God Taught Me

• God taught me that building real friendships, not superficial ones, is an important part of my spiritual growth.

• Although God is always with us, we need earthly reminders to help keep us on the right path. Authentic friendships are built on trust and respect. These kinds of friends don't just watch you grow as a Christian; they help you by praying for you, challenging you, and holding you accountable.

• Friendships that have Christ as their foundation have depth and meaning. They're worth an investment of time and energy.

Write Your Story

What could you do this week to be a better friend?

Talk to God

Use this prayer, or use your own words to talk to God.

Jesus, you set the example of the ideal friend. Your character is a perfect example for me, and you're working to make me more like you. I want to pursue real friendships. Help me be a friend to others. Amen.

Talk With Friends

Discuss these questions in a small group:

• Do you have a best friend right now? What makes that person such a good friend?

• What are the benefits of a Christian friendship? Does this kind of friend exist in your life? How has this kind of friend affected your life?

• How can you become a better friend to others?

Making Choices

Cameron's Story

I grew up in the church and tried to live my life for God, but as I got older, my life wandered further and further away from God. I wanted to be loud and crazy and to live my life unrestrained. My parents didn't agree with me.

In ninth grade, I began to seek out the darker side of myself. I started to distance myself from my family, and I stopped doing things that would make me seem so innocent. I made new friends who soon got me into all kinds of bad stuff. I started smoking and drinking and began to lie to my parents about where I was going. It seems that I never talked to them except to fight with them over a curfew or my bad attitude. I began going to wild parties and experimenting with pot. At first I liked the feeling of freedom smoking pot gave me.

The truth is that deep inside I knew that what I was doing was wrong. All the lies, drugs, and drunken nights built up guilt inside me. I had strayed far from God, and I knew it. I was an empty shell, doing as I pleased, rebelling, and filling up my soul with more guilt and lies. I kept trying to convince myself that what I'd longed for all of these years, popularity and danger, was all there was to life. I was so wrong. Even smoking pot didn't make me happy after a while because I knew it was wrong and I shouldn't be doing it. I felt God calling out to me, urging me to stop and come to him. But I knew that turning to God would mean leaving all the seemingly fun stuff behind.

I continued to travel down the wrong path. I went to wild parties on Saturday nights and then to church on Sunday mornings, badly hung over and still reeking of pot and cigarette smoke. It wasn't long before people realized I had changed. I was no longer the positive example they had thought I was.

During one summer in high school, my parents found a new church for my family to attend. I went to it and found that I had an opportunity to make a new start in a place where no one knew me. I often felt guilty when I walked through the doors after a wild weekend of partying, but the people there showed they cared for me.

Soon I got involved in the youth activities and joined a small group with a few friends and a leader. The group took me in and made me feel loved and accepted from the start. They challenged me in many good ways. I could feel the Holy Spirit's presence and leading during prayer and worship, but I did my best to shut him out while I went on with my meaningless life. It got harder and harder, though, to live a double life. I felt so guilty and convicted about my lifestyle that I stopped drinking

"Create in me a pure heart, O God, and renew a steadfast spirit within me. Do not cast me from your presence or take your Holy Spirit from me. Restore to me the joy of your salvation and grant me a willing spirit, to sustain me" (Psalm 51:10-12).

and doing drugs and started to seek God.

I finally reached out my weak hands and took hold of God's strong arms that had been waiting for me all along. Slowly I grew to know and understand God. I began to pray and read the Bible every night. Over time, I gave my life completely to God. I vowed never to drink, smoke, or do drugs again. With this rebirth came forgiveness and an end to all the guilt that had piled up inside of me. I was a brand-new creation and a child of God.

It has been over a year since I gave my life to God. I haven't gone back to my old ways, and I can see how much God has been teaching and molding me. God will do amazing things in your life if you just give him a chance!

What God Taught Me

• No matter how hard my life may seem, I'm never alone and I'm never without God's guidance.

• God can use my past mistakes for good. My experience has allowed me to share my faith with many friends who are facing the same temptations.

• There is no greater way to live than in the hands of Jesus. He'll set you free from guilt, shame, and temptation.

Write Your Story

What is God saying to you about the choices you're making and where they're leading you? What changes do you need to make in your life?

Talk to God

Use this prayer, or use your own words to talk to God.

Jesus, I am amazed that you have given me a second chance. I would be so far away from you if not for your unconditional love. Thank you for not giving up on me. Sometimes I'm tempted and weak, but in you, I can do all things. Amen.

Talk With Friends

Discuss these questions in a small group:

• How does God help you when you feel tempted to make a bad choice?

• Does anyone hold you accountable and help you stay on the right path? If so, who is it? If not, how can you find such a person?

• Do you know someone who is in a bad situation and might need your help? What could you do to offer assistance or encouragement?

Just Once

Lauren's Story

My life had become so routine that every day seemed like the one before. I would wake up at 6:30; go to school; go to volleyball practice; and then, on most nights, go straight to the student ministry at my church. I would get home around 9:30, do my homework, and then go to bed. Things were going pretty well: I was a starter on the volleyball team, my grades were good, and I had a great boyfriend. Yet because I was a freshman in high school, I felt I needed to branch out and make some new friends. I have a twin sister, and we've always had the same friends. They were starting to bore me.

I began socializing with a few juniors and seniors. Life was going great. But then every night I would find myself on the phone, talking to my new friends. I would lose track of time and fall asleep without studying for my tests or reading my Bible and praying. I felt guilty about not spending time with God because my friends and family had always considered me to be a good Christian girl. I used to bring my Bible to school and read it there, and all my old friends knew I was a Christian. But I just didn't feel like doing that anymore.

Since I was so busy with my new, older friends, my relationships with my parents and siblings suffered. Things weren't right. I wasn't doing life with God; I was doing it on my own. I'd go through mood swings and treat my friends and boyfriend badly. On Sunday mornings at church, I pretended that everything was fine. I continued to go to church and lead band for the junior high group and attend the high school ministry. I knew I was being a "Sunday Christian."

At school, I started noticing that a lot of my friends were involved with drugs and alcohol. It seemed that everyone was smoking pot. Lots of people were doing it every morning before school, and they seemed to have a lot of fun together. I had been against smoking pot my whole life, but I was very weak in my faith, and the Evil One threw a temptation my way that I couldn't pass up.

One day before school, a group of students was smoking pot in a hidden corner of the school. They asked me to join them, and I did. They handed me the pipe and told me how to take a hit. I didn't really want to do it, but I did because I was curious.

I didn't like pot at all, and it was the stupidest thing I've ever done. Trust me, if you ever want to try it just once, don't! I was amazed at how quickly I could make such a poor choice.

A couple of days went by, and I kept this sin hidden from everyone around me. But the sin grew in me, and it felt terrible. I thought constantly about what I had done, and I knew I had to tell someone because I felt so bad. Since I knew God is all-knowing, I confessed my sin to him and asked him to use this mistake to teach me a lesson. But I knew I also needed to confess my sin to a few close friends I could trust.

When Sunday morning rolled around, I went to church and met with my small group. We were taking turns telling about our week, and when my turn came, I asked God to give me strength to be honest with my friends and to deal with the consequences.

"I have to be honest with all of you," I said. "The other day at school, I smoked pot. But the good news is that I've confessed it to God and because of Christ, I've been forgiven."

I felt as if a huge weight had been lifted off my shoulders. My friends showed me understanding and love and helped me see some of the things that had led me to make such a poor choice.

> **"The Lord is slow to anger, abounding in love and forgiving sin and rebellion. Yet he does not leave the guilty unpunished"** (Numbers 14:18a).

The Holy Spirit was pushing me to confess this sin to my parents as well. I finally did, and though I was punished and grounded, the experience was good for me. I spent some needed quality time with my family. God showed me the rewards of telling the truth and striving to live with integrity.

What God Taught Me

• God is forgiving and loving. He wants me to regularly come to him with any problems or temptations I'm facing.

• God has used my poor decisions to teach me valuable life lessons.

• Honestly confessing to others helped bring healing to my soul.

• I was able to share my faith with my friends because they were able to see God working in my life.

Write Your Story

Are there any areas in your life in which you have been dishonoring God? Do you need to get back on track spiritually? Take time to write about your concerns and struggles, asking God to give you strength.

Talk to God

Use this prayer, or use your own words to talk to God.

Jesus, I need you to come first in all areas of my life. Help me not to be so busy with school, sports, or friends that I neglect you. Remind me that each step I take away from you makes it harder to make the right choices when social pressures come my way. Surround me with the right friends who will keep me accountable in my walk with you. Amen.

Talk With Friends

Discuss these questions in a small group:

• As a Christian, have you ever felt bored, as if you're missing out on all the fun? If so, why? If not, what keeps you excited about being a Christian?

• How are your priorities affecting your walk with God? Are the activities and friendships you're involved in bringing you closer to God or pushing you further away?

• What pressures and struggles are you facing right now? What change can you make this week that will enable you to handle them? How can the rest of the group support you right now?

Tired of Waiting
Rachel's Story

Every week it seemed I had a new crush on a different guy at school. The guys never seemed to like me back, and I always ended up alone. After being rejected so many times, I began to hate myself. At one point, my depression was so severe that I thought the end of my life would be a blessing to me and to everyone else. Why couldn't I get a boyfriend? How could I be that ugly? How much longer would I have to wait for someone?

All my friends were dating, which made the situation seem much worse. While they went out on dates on Saturday night, I was often alone at home. All my dating friends gave me the same speech: "Rachel, you are beautiful not only on the outside, but you're beautiful on the inside, too." Yeah, right! It never made me feel better. I was tired of waiting and being patient.

Why was I being tortured like this? One night at a party, I found yet another guy I could fall in love with. As usual, I turned on the charm with jokes that made everyone in the room laugh.

"Hey," I thought, "he said he likes my jokes—he must really like me!" I got a chance to talk with him and thought things were going well. But later that night, I found out he had hit on my best friend and asked for her number. What? How could that be? He was laughing at my jokes! Why didn't he want my number?

> "**Trust in the Lord and do good; dwell in the land and enjoy safe pasture. Delight yourself in the Lord and he will give you the desires of your heart**" (Psalm 37:3-4).

As usual, I went into a spiral of despair. After being rejected yet again, my heart felt crushed. I talked with a Christian friend soon after that, and she suggested that maybe God was trying to teach me a lesson about real love. She reminded me that God loves me and is the only one who can fill the void in my heart. She said that maybe God wants all of my heart.

What God Taught Me

• When God is ready for me to date, so am I. I trust him fully in this area.

• God completes me, and no boyfriend could ever do that. God is the only one who can fill my heart completely.

• I need to spend time developing my character and becoming more like Jesus.

Write Your Story

It's true! God loves you, and his love is perfect. Read 1 Corinthians 13, and be reminded that this is the kind of love God has for you. What needs do you want God to fill so you feel totally loved?

Talk to God

Use this prayer, or use your own words to talk to God.

Jesus, thank you for knowing my heart and all my needs. You've promised that you'll give me the desires of my heart. Show me how I'm trying to be fulfilled and satisfied apart from you. Amen.

Talk With Friends

Discuss these questions in a small group:

• What do you have a hard time waiting for? How has God tested your patience in the past week?

• When has a relationship become more important to you than God? What did you do about it?

• How can you make God your number-one priority?

Three's a Crowd
Heather's Story

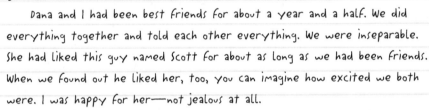

Last year, one of the worst things in my life happened: My best friend got a boyfriend. I know that shouldn't be such a big deal, but it was for me.

Dana and I had been best friends for about a year and a half. We did everything together and told each other everything. We were inseparable. She had liked this guy named Scott for about as long as we had been friends. When we found out he liked her, too, you can imagine how excited we both were. I was happy for her—not jealous at all.

When they started going out, Dana and I still did most things together. If Scott was there, it wasn't a problem. You know the saying "Two's company; three's a crowd"? That didn't apply to our situation at all. During the first two months, Dana was her usual fun, caring, and sensitive self. She was there for me when my grandmother went into the hospital and when my aunt and uncle divorced.

But this group of three worked only for a few months. Three started to become a crowd. I felt like an extra, unwanted and unneeded. Dana stopped calling me as often, and when she did call, all she wanted to talk about was Scott. It seemed as though she didn't want to hear what was going on in my life. I felt hurt and confused, as if I was losing my best friend to a guy.

I didn't tell her what was going on inside my confused head; I tried to act as I normally did when I was around her. I kept all that emotion bottled up and often felt as if I was going to explode. I started to back away from her and avoided her whenever possible.

One Sunday at church, it happened. She had been teasing me about a guy, and I had told her to stop, but suddenly I blew up. I walked out of the room and upstairs to the bathroom. I cried so hard. Some of my other friends came to see what was wrong, and I finally shared my struggles about Dana with them. Dana and I left church without speaking to each other.

Thinking about this now, I feel bad for Dana. She had no idea what was going on, and she was just as hurt and confused as I was. I wrote her a letter that week, explaining everything that had been going on inside my head for the past few months. We finally talked about it, and after we shed a few more tears, I thought our relationship would return to normal. But even though we called each other, our friendship wasn't the same.

I finally realized that I hadn't forgiven her. I didn't trust her and didn't want to be hurt again. She started ignoring me again, and I became just as confused as the first time. One day, I wrote this in my journal: "Sometimes I feel that I'll never be able to trust Dana again. She hurt me so badly. She still ignores me, and I'm afraid that things will never go back to the way they were. I don't want to push myself into that situation again if both of us are going to be hurt. I need her friendship, but I can't bring myself to fully trust her. I hate this feeling, and I wonder if I have really forgiven her. I just don't know."

> "Be kind and compassionate to one another, forgiving each other, just as in Christ God forgave you" (Ephesians 4:32).

I wrote her another letter and put our relationship in God's hands. Through a lot of conversations and prayer, we finally forgave each other. God gave me peace about what had happened, and we are best friends again.

What God Taught Me

• God taught me a lot about the importance of communication. I had just assumed that Dana would know what was going on in my mind.

• God wants us to deal with anger and hurt feelings right away.

• I can't be possessive of friends. I had to be able to give Dana a little space to spend time with other friends—it didn't mean she didn't care about me.

• Forgiveness is very important. God's desire to forgive us is so great that he sent his Son to die for us. During this hard time with Dana, I was reminded that God wants me to forgive as well so I can show his love to others.

Write Your Story

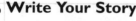

Jesus knows how you feel when a friend lets you down. He was let down by his friends, the disciples. When he was arrested in the garden of Gethsemane and needed support, all the disciples ran away (see Mark 14:50). If you're in a situation like Heather's, tell God what you're feeling. If you're not facing a tough issue with a friend, thank God for that special friendship.

Talk to God

Use this prayer, or use your own words to talk to God.

Jesus, people often let me down. Friends and family don't always have time for me, and my relationships aren't always what I want them to be. Help me understand that your love for me is perfect. Allow me to be a better friend to the people you've placed in my life. Thank you for being the kind of friend who will never disappoint me. Amen.

Talk With Friends

Discuss these questions in a small group:

• How does honest communication keep your friendships strong?

• When have you experienced a broken relationship? How did you feel?

• How has God shown you ways to handle broken relationships?

Out of Control
Justin's Story

In seventh grade I met new friends who stuck by me like glue. I couldn't wait to show them off to my old friends. These new friends loved to party, and because I was now a part of the group, I never turned down a drink or any kind of drug. I partied with them to be cool and accepted.

The partying turned from fun to a place of refuge when my parents got a divorce the next year. I continued this lifestyle for the next few years and into high school.

I turned to drinking exclusively after using drugs became dangerous and expensive. Drinking made me feel at peace. It was great fun, but then I started drinking all the time. I drank while driving to a friend's house and before I went to bed. I drank just to get drunk and as a way to escape. It became an addiction, meaningless and out of control. I felt that I was headed for death. I gave up on myself and felt I had no reason to live.

In the midst of all my drinking, a friend at school reached out to me and invited me to go to church with her. I laughed at her and asked her if she was joking. I had better things to do with my time than to go to some church event that would just tell me the way I was living my life was wrong. I wasn't happy with my life, but I sure didn't need someone else to point it out.

But for some reason, I decided to give it a try. My friend's student ministry was holding an event for people who "didn't know God." I felt uncomfortable being in a church, but I tried to be open. We started to sing, and I was amazed when I looked around and saw high school students singing to a God that was real to them. I could tell that worship was making them more joyful, peaceful, and excited about living life for God.

> "Then you will know the truth, and the truth will set you free…So if the Son sets you free, you will be free indeed" (John 8:32, 36).

I knew right then that I wanted feelings of peace and joy like those the students around me were experiencing. As soon as we were finished singing, the pastor talked about Jesus and how he came to earth to teach us and died to pay for our sins. He asked an important question that made me reflect on my own life: "What are you living for?" I could answer that question easily: "Nothing." That night, I made a decision to live my life for something, and that something is Jesus Christ.

What God Taught Me

• God has made a huge difference in my life! I wish I had made God the center of my life sooner, but I know he allowed me to make my own decisions, which led to some hard times. These experiences gave me the opportunity to grow closer to him in my pain and suffering.

• God's love for me will never change.

• God gave me hope and strength in overcoming my addiction.

Write Your Story

Sometimes we feel bombarded with temptations, and it's hard to make good choices. In what area of your life do you feel tempted and need God's help? In what area of your life have you overcome temptation? Tell God about it here.

Talk to God

Use this prayer, or use your own words to talk to God.

Jesus, thank you for being powerful and willing to help me anytime I ask you. I know I can overcome any temptation if you are in my life. Teach me to rely on you and not on my own strength. I look to you to lead my life. Amen.

Talk With Friends

Discuss these questions in a small group:

• When have you been tempted to compromise your values and convictions in order to be accepted?

• What is your view on alcohol and drugs? Where do you draw the line on the use of alcohol? drugs? What does the Bible say about these decisions?

• If you had a friend struggling with addiction, what would you say or do?

Tell Your Story

I hope this book has encouraged you and reminded you that you aren't alone. The stories you just read are real-life stories from Christian students around the world who desire to grow in their relationship with God and who are trying hard to make choices that honor him.

You, too, might have a story that needs to be told, and I'd love to hear from you! Please send me your story so it can encourage others and possibly be included in the next student devotional.

Send your stories to

Bo Boshers

c/o Willow Creek Association

P.O. Box 3188

Barrington, IL 60011-3188

If you'd like, you can e-mail your story to me at boshersb@willowcreek.org. Please be sure to include your name, address, and phone number so I can get in touch with you!

Group Publishing, Inc.
Attention: Product Development
P.O. Box 481
Loveland, CO 80539
Fax: (970) 679-4370

Evaluation for
DOING LIFE WITH GOD

Please help Group Publishing, Inc. continue to provide innovative and useful resources for ministry. Please take a moment to fill out this evaluation and mail or fax it to us. Thanks!

● ● ●

1. As a whole, this book has been (circle one)

not very helpful   very helpful

| 1 | 2 | 3 | 4 | 5 | 6 | 7 | 8 | 9 | 10 |

2. The best things about this book:

3. Ways this book could be improved:

4. Things I will change because of this book:

5. Other books I'd like to see Group publish in the future: